Contents

"A heritage of the Lord"

Every christian couple marries with the hope that one day children will be born and they will enjoy a family of their own. In some cases it is not the Lord's will that this should be so, but to marry with the avowed intention of preventing the birth of any children is contrary to the teaching of Scripture and must never be contemplated by those who mean to honour the Lord in their marriage.

Much is written today about how children should be brought up. Parents who have seen their children grow from babies to mature adults realise that the approach to parenthood when a child is young and dependent upon its parents is very different from what is necessary when the child becomes a teenager. In their teens, sons and daughters may begin to feel independent of their parents, and may begin to form views which are opposed to what they have been taught. These views may be somewhat extreme because of lack of experience and maturity. This booklet deals mainly with the early years of a child's life, although most of the principles apply at all times. The particular problems of the teenage years are dealt with in a separate booklet in this series.

God who gives children will provide for their support

Society today has calculated how much it will cost to bring up a child until it is independent of its parents. Clothes, schooling, food, heat, light, holidays, and every other cost is taken into account - until a figure is arrived at which seems almost beyond the reach of the ordinary family! This calculation is to make you consider whether you can afford to have children, but it loses sight of the fact that the God who gives children will provide for their support when we acknowledge Him in our lives. We are also told that the birth of children must not disturb the even tenor of parents' lives, and that a mother should continue her employment, placing her children in the care of others, even when the necessities of life could easily be provided without this. There may be pressing circumstances which make this situation necessary, and where it is unavoidable the Lord will make up for the distress which a mother feels in having to go out to work. But where economic demands can be reduced to enable a mother to be with her children, christian parents with spiritual desires will see that this is what happens. They will not yield to the pressures of our materialistic society, fuelled by the media and by the accepted 'wisdom' of our day which makes motherhood a second best choice for a wife with no desire to realise her true potential. By adopting a life-style which a husband's income alone cannot support, a mother loses the most important privilege given to a wife, that of rearing her own children.

See children born and watch them grow

As a result of these pressures, children nowadays are often spoken of as if they were a burden which restricts the life of their parents. Their cost is calculated clinically and they are regarded as the means of destroying the mother's career. Scripture, however, treats them in an entirely different light: "Children are an heritage of the Lord" (Psalm 127:3)!

It is one of the greatest blessings of married life to see children born and to watch them grow from being babies, entirely dependent on others, to the stage where they are completely independent. These years of physical, emotional, intellectual, and, we trust, spiritual development are not only a time of education for the children, but also for parents. Great lessons can be learned as the needs of children are met, needs which differ with the passing years. In Scripture, spiritual growth is likened to a child's growth, and observant parents will note with interest these various stages of growth and will be able to draw spiritual lessons from them for themselves.

A time of education also for parents

Thus the birth of children is a great blessing from the Lord, and surely should not be regarded as an imposition of an economic penalty impacting the social life of the parents. With the coming of a family the pattern of life will change, but it will have its own richness and yield its own rewards.

The first question to ask

It was a dark time in the history of Israel. The conduct of the people was evil, for they had turned their backs on the Lord. The Philistines had invaded the land and for a period of forty years held the Israelites in bondage. These were not good years through which to live, and many may have considered that it was a bad time to bring children into the world.

How shall we order the child?

In the tribe of Dan there was one childless family who, despite the times, were anxious to have a child. Doubtless their inability to have children was the source of much grief, and the godlessness of the age was no consolation. To the grieving wife, however, there came an angel one day with the welcome news that she would conceive and give birth to a son. Her joy was overflowing, and she hurries to bring the news to her husband, Manoah. Like all responsible husbands, he was concerned that the child should be brought up properly, so when the angel appears to him he asks the question which should be on the lips of all parents who wish to honour the Lord: "How shall we order the child, and how shall we do unto him?" (Judges 13:12).

This question is as important today as when it was first asked. For all parents, children will occupy their attention for a great part of their married life, and will be dependent on them for many years. They will love them, sacrifice for them, train them, and above all ensure that, as christian parents, they teach them the gospel and the Word of God.

In carrying out the work of parenthood it is vital to commence and continue with due attention to the Scriptures. There are countless theories propounded and books written on the subject of bringing up children, but christian parents will still turn to the Lord and to His Word to learn the answer to this vital question. Only there can trustworthy advice be found.

Turn to the Lord and to His word

It is interesting to note that the answer received by Manoah was, firstly, that his wife must obey the Word of God. She had been told how to conduct herself in the months before the child was born and this is re-stated to her husband. The first basic lesson on parenthood is thus driven home, that those to whom is entrusted the care and upbringing of children must themselves determine to obey the Scriptures. There is no sense in expecting children to put the Word of God into practice in their lives, if their parents show no signs of doing so. Parents' submission to the word of the Lord does not commence when the children are in their teens or when they reach the so-called age of responsibility. For Manoah and his wife this must be the character of their life from now on, even before the birth of their child.

The responsibilities of parenthood

Before examining the subject more closely we should note that there are three general statements found in the Bible which summarise the responsibilities of parenthood.

1. The responsibility to train up the child

"Train up a child in the way he should go" (Prov 22:6).

Their first priority ... spiritual training

It has often been remarked that there are two ways in which a child may develop: the way that he would go and the way that he should go. Christian parents will have as their first priority the spiritual training of their children, which like all training, will take place over the years, not in a few days or weeks. In this training, example will be a prime means of instruction, backed up by instruction from the Word of God suited to the age of the child. Bringing up a child on 'freedom of self- expression' or 'self-development' is a modern concept which not only leads to noisy, disruptive children, but also ignores the fact that we are all born with a rebellious, sinful nature. It is an act of parental irresponsibility to allow that nature to develop unchecked.

2. The responsibility to bring up the child

"Bring them up in the nurture and admonition of the Lord" (Eph 6:4).

Parents must not bring up their children in an atmosphere of fear and confrontation. This approach will only provoke them to wrath (Col 3:21). They must be brought up, rather, in the nurture and admonition of the Lord. Thus, although children have to be nurtured, that is rebuked and chastised, they must also be admonished, which is correction mixed with encouragement. The child must not be treated in a way which gives the impression that he or she is constantly doing what is wrong. This will destroy all self-confidence and create resentment. Where possible, encouragement must be given, even when correction is necessary.

Correction mixed with encouragement

3. The responsibility to lay up for the child

"...for the children ought not to lay up for the children, but the parents for the children" (2 Cor 12:14).

Here Paul is not teaching that parents must lay up a store of material wealth for their children to inherit. That would be advice completely contrary to the words of the Lord Jesus: "Lay not up for yourselves treasures upon earth" (Matt 6:19). Parents, however, are to fulfil their obligations in meeting the cost of bringing up their children. They must accept that it falls to them to meet the needs of their children until they come to maturity and are able to maintain themselves. The exhortation is, therefore, not to accumulate material wealth, but to meet the daily cost of bringing up a family.

The following pages will set out more fully the teaching of Scripture on parenthood, and will show that the desire to bring up children in a God-honouring way must be backed up, above all, by an acknowledgement of the Lordship of Christ in the lives of the parents. Only then can we sincerely ask the question, "How shall we order the child?"

The Lordship of Christ in the lives of the parents

Children and their home

What kind of home should christian parents provide for their children? It is worth looking at how the Bible describes the home.

The home is a nursery.

"We were gentle among you, even as a nurse cherisheth her children" (1 Thess 2:17).

In describing his attitude to those young Christians in Thessalonica, Paul states that he was gentle among them as a nurse, that is a nursing mother, took care of her own children. The picture is not of a mother hiring a nurse to take care of her children, but rather the mother herself caring for them.

Here we have good advice about the care of those who are very young. The mother has to treat her children in a gentle, placid, tolerant way. We will see that this does not mean that they have not to be disciplined, and thus become annoying to those who find themselves in their company. It does mean that the mother has not to be constantly irritated, angry and annoyed at her children. Mothers know that this is not an easy task, as children can try a mother's patience to the limit, but the mother who loves and cares for her children will have a tolerant way with them which is often a marvel to those who look on.

Protects them from the cold winds of ungodly influences

In the home the mother cherishes her children. She keeps them warm and protects them from the cold winds of ungodly influences. In these early years it will be her ambition to ensure that they are protected as much as possible, so that the impressions left with them are of godliness and devotion to the Lord Jesus. In the verse which follows the one quoted above Paul states that he was willing even to have given his own soul for them. His well-being was secondary to the well-being of these believers young in the faith. So, likewise, a loving mother guards her children and her well-being is, to her, of secondary importance compared to the well-being of her child.

This vital part of motherhood cannot be carried out effectively if the child is given over into the care of others for the greater part of the day. The modern tendency to expect a mother to return to work shortly after the birth of her child and look to grandparents or child-minders to care for the child during the day, is no substitute for the time, love and attention which a mother gives. There may be especially trying situations where a mother has unwillingly to take this course, and in such a situation the Lord will take care of the child. But where this is done to attain a standard of living which is beyond the financial ability of the husband to maintain, the spiritual couple will decide before the Lord to bring their standard of living within the limits of the husband's income and take proper care of the child which the Lord has given them.

The prime role of a mother is caring for her children

It may be argued that the material benefits which the child enjoys because of the mother's income far outweigh any disruption caused by both parents being at work all day. This shows a lack of appreciation of the vital part which a mother plays in the bringing up of the child. It also reveals a failure to acknowledge that the prime role of a mother is to be responsible for the day to day work of caring for her children.

The home is an academy.

"And that from a child thou hast known the holy scriptures, which are able to make thee wise unto salvation through faith which is in Christ Jesus" (2 Tim 3:15).

The mother and grandmother of Timothy were Christians, and they set out early in Timothy's life to teach him the Holy Scriptures.

When Timothy was a child these consisted of the Old Testament scriptures. It is clear that in this home they were given a prominent place.

From a very early age, therefore, Timothy was introduced to the Book. It may be that he was taught to read and write by tracing out these sacred words. Little wonder, therefore, that he came to know them intimately. They were impressed on his mind from the beginning and became part of him. He and the Scriptures could not be separated.

Christian parents do not leave this most vital part of their children's education to the schools which they attend. It will not be left either to the Sunday school which they will attend. The process of learning starts at the very beginning and has as its objective the introduction of children to the basic lessons of Scripture. At an early age they will be taught the stories and lessons to be found within its pages. The responsibility lies with the parents, and not with others, no matter how well qualified they may appear to be.

Never forget how retentive a young child's memory is

The objective in teaching the Scriptures is not to increase the child's knowledge, or to give it an early advantage over other children. What is on the hearts of the parents is that Scripture is able to make those who know it "wise unto salvation". By this means they will learn the great, all important, most fundamental lesson of all, that they are sinners, despite their young years, and that salvation is to be found in the Lord Jesus alone. We must never forget how retentive a young child's memory is.

A day will come when the child commences school and will come under the influence of teachers who, no matter how professional and well meaning in their efforts, may teach what is contrary to your beliefs. Evolution is one such subject which is taught as a proven fact to children from an early age. When faced with this situation some parents may decide that their children should not be part of the class when this is being taught. This can be one solution, but it is not always possible and may create further problems for the child at school. What parents must do in this situation is ensure that the sound, careful teaching of the Scriptures at home counters the false teaching received elsewhere. Remember in your dealings with schools that the teachers involved who are unbelievers will themselves have accepted as fact what they are teaching, and will not be going out of their way to teach what they know to be error. This will give you the opportunity of explaining your beliefs to them in a way which will commend the gospel.

How important it is in the home that children are not exposed continually to children's programs in the media, and to all the books and literature which are available, without the Bible being given first place. Just as the parents of Moses preserved him in the ark of bulrushes, and as his mother nursed him and taught him when he was taken into the court of Pharaoh, and by so doing laid the foundations of a life which would be lived in the service of God, so today it falls to all christian parents to guard and teach their children with a view to laying the foundations of a life which they pray will be devoted to the service of the Master. They are looking ahead, if the Lord will, to the day when, in adult life, they become mature and "fully furnished to all good works". Blessed indeed are those children whose parents understand that the process of preparing them for His service starts at the beginning of their days. It is not a guarantee that the children will be saved, but it is the fulfilment of the responsibility placed on the shoulders of all christian parents.

laying the foundations of life

The home is a sanctuary.

"For this child I prayed...Therefore also I have lent him to the Lord" (1 Sam 2:27-28).

It is a fundamental principle in the raising of children that they should be brought up in the atmosphere of the sanctuary. The home will be a place where the Lord Jesus is honoured and His presence

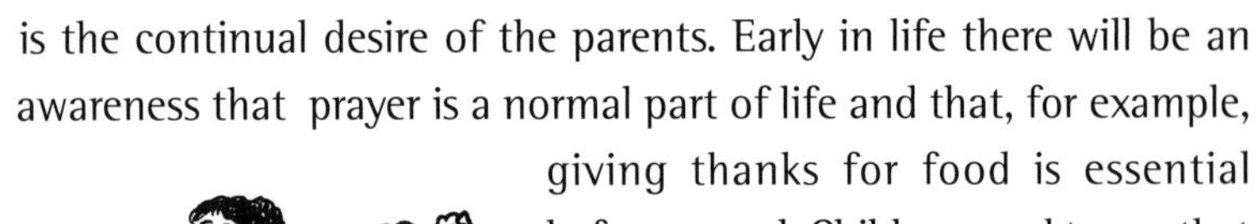

is the continual desire of the parents. Early in life there will be an awareness that prayer is a normal part of life and that, for example, giving thanks for food is essential before a meal. Children need to see that attendance to spiritual matters is not for Lord's Days alone, but is an integral part of daily life. We have seen that children should be taught the lessons of Scripture, but they must also see these lessons being put into practice.

The child given to Hannah was asked from the Lord in prayer. Her delight in bearing a son did not cause her to forget her responsibilities either towards the God who had answered her prayer or towards her son. She decided that at the earliest possible age he would be taken to Shiloh to be reared by those who attended the Tabernacle. Today it is not necessary to send children away to achieve this as our own homes can be a sanctuary for the bringing up of children.

Hannah's motive was clear. She observed the spiritual deterioration of her day and knew that a man of God was required to restore the nation to the Lord. Her desire was that her son should be a man fitted for such a momentous task. We now know that her faithful devotion was rewarded and the child grew to be one of the great leaders of Israel. On her part it required sacrifice, but she had a clear purpose in mind and would not be deflected from this by the sacrifice involved. This did not mean that Samuel's physical welfare was ignored. Each year she brought him a new coat, and took good care to ensure that all his needs were fully met.

Prayer is a normal part of life

Today there is still a great need for parents who are devoted to the Lord and who will devote their children to Him. The mother and father who look ahead, if the Lord will, to the adulthood of their children, and bring them up in a home where the presence of God is a reality, are laying good foundations for a later life of useful service to the Master. This is not a guarantee that they will come to know Him and serve Him, but it is fulfilling their responsibility as parents.

Foundations for a later life of useful service

The children need to know the difference which exists between their home and the homes of other children. Do ensure, however, that their home is not a joyless place of always being told 'no'. For every 'no' try to make sure that there is an acceptable 'yes' so that memories will remain of a home which was happy, of a childhood which was fulfilling, of parents who were caring, and of the central place which was given to the Lord. Give them memories of praying parents who committed them to the Lord, and let them learn early that the christian life is an attractive one.

Never let the poison of gossip come into this atmosphere. It is so easy for parents to forget the presence of their children, and indulge in conversation which is not profitable, speaking in a disparaging way about others in front of children who will retain memories of conversations which later you will wish that they had never heard.

Ensure also that matters which are not for young ears to hear are discussed only when children are out of earshot. They are too young to be introduced to subjects which may leave them with wrong impressions of the christian life.

The christian life is an attractive one

Children and their father

A father must deal individually.

"As ye know how we exhorted and comforted and charged every one of you" (1 Thess 2:11).

Each child is an individual. All have different personalities and differing needs. A father will recognise that each of his children must be treated in a way which is suited to his or her character. Perception on the part of the parents will be required to discern the differences between each child. When a child is born into a family where there are older children, it is important that the older ones do not feel that they are overlooked.

The father first of all exhorts his child. In doing this he is encouraging the child with a view to the future. There are many situations in life where encouragement is required, even when children are young. Any father who does not consider the future of his children is failing in his duty, but he must also recognise the encouragement necessary for the growth of the child spiritually, intellectually and in every other way.

The father also comforts the child. It may seem strange to see this task given to a father, as we would expect it rather to be undertaken by a mother. Consolation is necessary when circumstances become difficult. The father is showing that he is not only concerned with the future, but also has a concern about current difficulties and problems of life. Many of these concerns may seen insignificant to an adult, but to a child they seem enormous. What a help it can be when father takes time to console and to offer advice. This will help

Each child is an individual

the child to see the problems in perspective, and is valuable education for handling the difficulties which we all have to face.

A father rules admirably.

"One that ruleth well his own house" (1 Tim 3:4).

The father is the one with whom lies ultimate responsibility for the home. He is not, however, to be thought of as an autocratic figure whose every whim has to be obeyed and who treats the other members of his family as subservient to him. This falls very far short of New Testament teaching.

When Paul wrote the words above he was dealing with the qualifications required for working as an elder in the local church. This must not, however, be looked on as instructions for a small group of fathers who desire to carry out the work of an elder. It is God's pattern for every father, but those who fail to practise this exclude themselves from eldership.

He must not lose the respect of his children

A christian father will rule his house well. This means that he does so in an attractive manner, and not as we have seen, in an autocratic manner. It involves the father acting with gravity and dignity in all that he does. He must not lower this standard at any time and by so doing lose the respect of his children. Children must be able to respect their father and to recognise that he can be trusted and that he lives a consistent life. There is little point in teaching children how to live and then fail to practise what you teach.

We also learn that rule in the home falls ultimately on the father. It is true that the mother will discipline the children when it is necessary, but the father cannot escape his responsibility of ensuring that there is rule in the home. Children will therefore be taught that they are not free to do as they wish. They will be taught early in life the importance of discipline, that wrong doing is rewarded and that well doing is also rewarded. How vital it is that in the early years children become aware of this and recognise that rule does exist in the home.

Social problems today stem from unruly homes

This does not mean the imposition of impossible or outrageous restrictions. Children are children and must be allowed to act as children. No more must be expected of them. A home ruled according to the principles of the Scriptures is a good start for any life. So many of our social problems today stem from unruly homes where there is no authority.

To allow a child to develop without correction is to fail on a number of counts. It is not teaching the difference between what is right and what is wrong. It is failing to equip the child to deal with others, so that few will wish the company of such a child in early years, or as personality 'develops'. Above all it fails to teach the basic lessons of sin and salvation.

A father guides graciously.

"Fathers, provoke not your children to anger, lest they be discouraged" (Col 3:21).

Bringing up children can be a task which at times tries parents' patience to the limit. The constant repetition of warnings and the pleas to behave, followed by the continual noisy disobedience of the child, can make life so demanding that despair sometimes takes over.

It may be that in seeking to prevent this taking place, father is always admonishing the children, and stamps on any burst of energy which threatens to disturb the quiet atmosphere of the home. Eventually it may become the father's normal approach to place exacting demands upon his children and to constantly criticise all they do. Although this may have commenced with a good motive, it can become a habit, no matter what the child does.

As a child grows, a father may look in vain for the development of characteristics which he wishes to see in his children. Where these are not seen, no matter what other admirable characteristics are observed, the father can fall into the trap of treating his children as if they were unwilling to do as he wishes, and make it look as if they will grow into adults with no useful abilities. With some children these anxieties may be well justified. The child may not show any diligence at school and may exhibit few features that can be praised.

Encourage children at all times

Faced with these dangers, a father must be careful to ensure that he does not constantly irritate the child by continual blame for falling short of the father's expectations. He must not place on the child exacting demands which are beyond the child's ability to attain. Above all he must not expect the child to set his heart on his parents' ambitions, without taking the child's strong and weak points into account. It has been known for parents to try and live their lives through their children, wishing them to achieve objectives which were denied the parents in early life. The danger of discouraging children is very real when the child comes to feel that no matter what he or she does, the parents will never be pleased with the results. The child will feel deficient with no worthwhile abilities to develop.

The wise father will seek to encourage his children at all times. There will always be actions which can be praised, and wisdom demands that this be done whenever opportunity arises. As a result the child will accept warnings and rebuke more readily, knowing that the father is fair in his assessment.

As children grow, and if they begin to show interest in spiritual matters, the same care must be exercised. Young people cannot be expected to have spiritual views which are similar to those of more mature parents. Again ensure that commendation comes before condemnation. Encourage what can be encouraged and, when correction is needed, see that this is done graciously, making sure that your criticism is well founded and can be backed up by sound reasoning.

Commendation comes before condemnation

The father loves tenderly.

"Like as a father pitieth his children" (Psalm 103:13).

We have seen that the father's place in the home is one of ultimate responsibility for the ordering of the home and for any discipline which is necessary for the good of the children. It should be emphasised that a father must not be given to violence in carrying out these duties. Paul clearly tells us that he must be "no striker". He must not be feared by his children for his display of anger and violence.

It is possible that the father may be thought of as one who is involved in family life only when correction is necessary. This also must be avoided. The psalmist tells us that a father will show tender mercy towards his children. It is not that he pities them in the sense of thinking they are inadequate and pitying their poor performance or abilities. It is that he has a real affection and love for them and treats them with tender care. They are his children and he loves them because of that. If you read the following verse in Psalm 132 you will learn that as the father shows tender mercy towards his children "so the Lord pitieth them that fear Him". Here, then, is a great opportunity which is presented to a father. He can display to his children the same care and tender mercy which he has experienced from the Lord. To the young child he can impart a sense of the loving care which is part of real fatherhood, and give the child a living lesson in the great loving care of God.

Loving care is part of real fatherhood

Children watch their parents and observe closely how they behave. Their first lessons are in the home from observing their mother and father. Let them see from the beginning that tender mercy and loving care is an essential part of the father's role in the home.

Children and their mother

The relationship between a mother and a father and their children will differ in a number of important ways. They will not work against each other but will complement each other. It is vitally important to ensure that differences between parents are not aired in front of the children, but are discussed when the parents are alone. There must never be a time when a difference of opinion is seen to exist as to how the children should be treated or corrected. This would show the child that there is not a unity of view, and will lessen the respect which a child will have for its parents.

Let us examine what the Scripture has to say about a christian mother and her children.

She lives a godly life before them.

"I am thy servant and the son of thine handmaid" (Psalm 116:16).

"Save the son of thine handmaid" (Psalm 86:16).

The identity of the writer of Psalm 116 is not known to us, although we do know that it is not likely to be David. Psalm 86, however, was written by David. So here we have the testimony of two men that their mothers were godly women. Both of them, speaking to God, state that their mothers were "Thine handmaiden". The name of David's father is revealed, but not the name of his mother. These two mothers have not left their names for us, but they left deep impressions with their children. What a privilege it was to be brought up in a home where the mother was known for her godliness.

Mothers have left deep impressions with their children

To a mother is given the great responsibility of being with her children almost constantly from an early age. It is her influence at

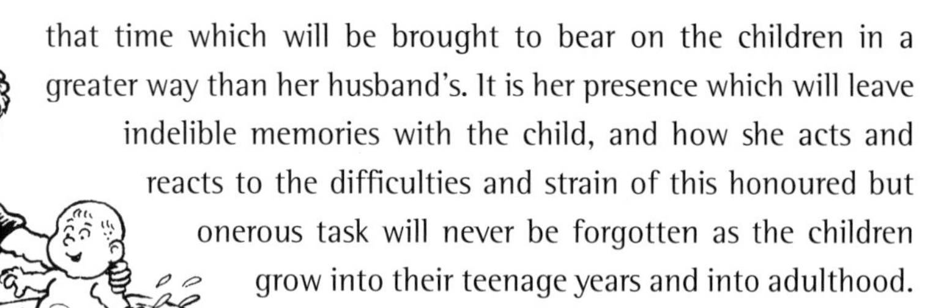

that time which will be brought to bear on the children in a greater way than her husband's. It is her presence which will leave indelible memories with the child, and how she acts and reacts to the difficulties and strain of this honoured but onerous task will never be forgotten as the children grow into their teenage years and into adulthood.

That these two mothers were faithful wives we have no doubt. We can also be very sure that they were good mothers in providing all that was necessary for the good of their children. The strongest impressions left with the children, however, was not of their relationship with their husbands, no matter how loving that relationship was, nor was it the care and attention which they as children enjoyed, but it was, rather, the devotion to the Lord seen daily and observed closely. In Psalm 123:2 we read, "Behold, as the eyes of servants look unto the hand of their masters and as the eyes of the maiden unto the hand of her mistress; so our eyes wait upon the Lord our God". The picture is of the hand-maiden sitting in the presence of her mistress looking intently at her, to act immediately when the hand of the mistress indicates that she has to come or to go, to fetch or to carry away. So these two mothers left deep impressions of being constantly in the presence of the Lord, waiting to act in obedience to His will, watching and listening for every indication of what He would have them to do. Is not this the first fundamental lesson which a christian mother and father would teach their children?

How she acts and reacts will never be forgotten

She protects them.

"As a hen gathered her chickens under her wings" (Matt 23:37).

These words were spoken by the Lord Jesus as He looked down on Jerusalem and sorrowed because of that city's refusal to come to Him. The illustration of a hen gathering her chickens under her wing is a beautiful picture of protectiveness which a mother feels for her children and of her actions in seeking to preserve them from what is harmful.

There is much in the world today from which children need to be protected, and the mother must be with them to ensure that they are not exposed to what is harmful. We know that there are dangers outside of the home where evil men and women can prey upon children, and it is clear that protection from that danger is vital.

They are not exposed to what is harmful

Less obvious, however, are the dangers to which children can be exposed unwittingly. The media are a source of such danger, and what children see and hear must be carefully vetted at all times. Always remember that the standards by which christian parents judge such matters are not the standards of the world. Even what the world states is acceptable may be completely unacceptable to those who have a care for the spiritual well-being of their children.

Our illustration from the words of the Lord Jesus gives us a picture of a watchful mother, ever careful of the well-being of the children she loves, and gathering them close to her to keep them safe. She is unconcerned about the danger to herself, but hides her children where no harm can come to them. Such is the love of a true mother.

She is an example of industry to them.

"....and eateth not the bread of idleness. Her children arise and call her blessed" (Prov 31:28).

This may seem a strange feature to introduce here, but it is a vital part of the training of children. We have already seen how important is the example of parents to their children. The mother here is seen to have a particularly important part to play in teaching the child the value of work well carried out and honestly done.

The work of a housewife is a full time job which requires all the hours of the day to carry it out. With a house to be kept, meals to be made, washing to be done, children to be cared for, and all the other tasks which have to be performed, a busy mother has little time for herself. The early impression of industrious effort is a good impression to leave with children. It must not be thought that this task is a second rate way of life which is only open to those who have no legitimate ambitions in life. Far from it. The responsibility of running a home and bringing up children is of prime importance and requires effort and energy to be completed satisfactorily.

When children see a mother spending large parts of every day in bed 'resting', or wasting time when work has to be done, they are being taught wrong lessons and are being left with memories which will surface in later days when they are urged to work harder or apply greater energy to school work etc. The mother who eats the bread of idleness cannot complain when a child grows up to do likewise.

Her industrious attention has proved her love

If you read the earlier verses in Proverbs 31 you will find a beautiful description of a virtuous women. This woman is, in the estimation of that writer, priceless. She cares for all aspects of the life of the home and neglects nothing. She is responsible for food for the household, for clothes for the family; she cares for the poor who live round about her, and she labours far into the night to see that all possible needs are satisfied. No wonder her children rise up and call her blessed, because her industrious attention to all their needs has proved her love for them. This mother has earned the respect and affection of her family, and in later days they will remember her devotion.

Examples of good parenthood

Preserving children from the world

"...she hid him three months" (Exod 2:2).

The mother of Moses was well aware that her son had been born into a hostile world. The command of Pharaoh put the life of every male child in danger, but this godly woman determined that her son would be preserved. To ensure that Moses would come to no harm she hid him at home for three months, and when this was no longer possible she made an ark of bulrushes and hid him in the reeds which were growing beside the river Nile.

Godly parents will be concerned for their children

This illustrates how godly parents will be concerned for their children where there is an enemy who is all out to ensure that the child will not possess eternal life. This enemy desires only harm for the young, and knowing this, godly parents will hide their young child from this adversary.

There comes a time, however, when the child no longer can be kept in the home, but must go out to face the world. Once again the godly mother has been at work, and when the child goes she has ensured that all the required protection has been made available to it. She did not want her son to be lost in the world's river.

Into circumstances like this God comes and shows that He also has a care for the child. Help is found from the most unlikely source, the palace of Pharaoh. In all that follows we see clearly that the Lord has a plan for the life of this child, and He will preserve him until the day comes when he will take up his great enterprise of leading the Israelites out of Egypt towards the land of Canaan.

God also has a care for the child

As the mother hid the child carefully in her home, as she prepared the ark and as she instructed her daughter Miriam to keep watch over the ark in the river, she little knew that she was carrying out a task which was vital for the future blessing of the Israelites. How many mothers have guarded their children from the influences of a wicked world and from the attention of the enemy whose desire is to possess them, little knowing that her child would grow to be a mighty man or woman in the service of the Lord. This woman could have decided that the risks and effort required were too great for her. She could surely leave this to someone else and submit to the edict of Pharaoh, arguing that she could not put the lives of her husband and the other members of her family at risk! Could it not be that she had in view the need for a future Deliverer of the people when she desired to have another child? The birth of Moses was not just an event which brought joy into that family, it was not only the birth of a son with whom in future they could share the joys of growing and maturing; it was the birth of a child who could be taught about the God of Israel and who could be fitted to become of great value to His people. May all christian parents have similar desires for their children.

A task vital for future blessing

Providing for growth

"Moreover his mother made him a little coat, and brought it to him from year to year" (1 Sam 2:19).

The child which had been given to Hannah by the Lord was in turn given back to the Lord by Hannah. As with the case of the mother of Moses we believe that Hannah had more in mind than simply satisfying her desire to have a son of her own. Her desires went beyond that, as she recognised that a man was needed in Israel to right the wrongs which she saw around her and to establish once again the spiritual life of the nation. Thus it was that, after some years, she took the child to Eli the priest, and Samuel grew up at Shiloh surrounded by all that reminded him of the great glorious days of the past, and the sad losses of their present failure.

Each year Hannah came up to Shiloh and brought with her a little coat. The child was growing and what had been appropriate last year was no longer adequate. So Hannah, each year, fitted her work to the age and growth of her son. Happy is the mother who is able to recognise the changing needs of a child as it grows and develops. It is sad to see a child who is unable to develop, but it is also sad to see a mother who is not able to recognise changes which are taking place, and who wishes to keep her family always as young children, dependent on her for everything. This may be the result of the mother feeling that she needs to be needed, but it will lead to immaturity in the children.

Recognise the changing needs of a child

It is equally sad to see parents who try to 'force' their children with ideas that they are intellectually ahead of children of the same age. This may stem from a genuine desire to see a child mature and get on, but it may also stem from a false sense of pride, claiming that their child is more intellectually gifted than others. Recognise the danger in both courses of action! Neither leads to healthy, normal development in your family.

Hannah's concern was that the child should always wear what suited his age. He must always be seen to have the maturity fitted to the years he has lived, and neither be 'too young' or 'too old'. Thus young children must play as young children will. They must be given what is of interest to them, and not be expected to read and show interest in what is beyond their years. Similarly, they must not be held back by a refusal to accept that they are growing and will gradually become independent of their parents. Make sure that the coat is changed when necessary and always fits the child.

Praying for new life

"She... laid him on the bed....and said, Send me, I pray thee...that I may run to the man of God" (2 Kings 4:21-22).

In the book of Kings we are introduced to one of the most remarkable women of the Bible. She notes that Elisha, the man of God, passes her house frequently, and arranges that accommodation is set aside for him in the guest room of her house. That she is a woman of great spiritual perception can be seen in her recognition of Elisha as a holy man of God. That she had desires to be engaged in furthering the work of God is seen in the welcome which she gave Elisha into her home.

The prophet tests her by offering her the reward of position in the palace or with the governing classes of the kingdom, but she responds by stating firmly that she wishes to dwell among her own people. She had no desire for promotion in the world. Then the prophet promises her a child, and in spite of how unlikely this appeared to be, the child is born in fulfilment of the promise.

Your desires for the spiritual well-being of your children

But after some years the child dies and his mother must go to find Elisha. The boy's father cannot understand why his wife would wish to go and see the man of God when it was not a time for religious feasts or observances. He had a complete lack of spiritual interests and limited his dealings with God to particular days. Not for him daily involvement in spiritual matters. Not for him seasons of prayer for the child when he was ill. It was the boy's mother who was in touch with God.

So this concerned spiritual woman hurries to meet Elisha and seek his help in raising her son to life again. After the prophet prays and agonises over the child, life returns to him again and the woman has the joy of her child with her, alive and well. This woman prayed that her child might be delivered out of death and be given new life. Here is a picture of the desire of a parent that a child would be delivered from death. Today deliverance from spiritual death is the desire of all christian parents for their children.

The education and advancement of your family in the world is not the prime concern of life. Let your desires be for the spiritual well-being of your children and come constantly in prayer to ask the Lord that they will be saved to enjoy new life, eternal life, which is given to all who believe the gospel. Parents who seek only material objectives will have difficulty in later years convincing their children that they should have other priorities. It will seem hypocritical to tell your family to pursue spiritual ambitions if for many years you pursued other things. This Shunnamite woman refused material advancement when it was offered to her.

You cannot guarantee that your prayers will result in the salvation of your children, but like so many other issues involved in the rearing of a family, you will know that you did all that you could to lead them in right paths.

The response of children

The responsibility to obey parents

"Children obey your parents in all things: for this is well pleasing to the Lord" (Col 3:20).

It is good practice to teach children early in life the importance of obedience. We have already alluded to the practice of allowing children 'self-expression'. This has become fashionable because of the false argument that any form of chastening or discipline is harmful to the development of the child. The result is a child who is unpleasant and forward, with no understanding of how a child should behave or of the bad impression which it leaves with others.

Christians realise that obedience is necessary for the full development of character. For the believer obedience to the Word of God is vital, and rather than stifle growth, it is necessary to bring about healthy growth. Parents, therefore, who seek the best for their children will bring them up ensuring that they are not disobedient. Often mothers and fathers of children who are ill taught and disobedient fail to recognise the effect which their family is having on others. Some parents cannot see any faults in their own children.

Obedience is necessary for the full development of character

Obedience, however, has not to be based on adherence to unreasonable demands, nor on a life-style which treats the child as an encumbrance and insists that it remains quiet constantly. A child must not gain the impression that any request made to its parents is an unwelcome interruption to their lives.

The child must be taught to obey the basic principles of Scripture. This includes the need for honesty, consideration for others, respect for those who are older, and the fact that they are responsible for the consequences of their actions. Sudden and regular outbursts of anger showing the parents to have lost self-control is not the way to bring this about. The child should be taught to live as the parents live. A child will be quick to discern when what is being demanded of them is not put into practice by others.

At times it will be necessary to chastise the child. To fail to do so is not the act of a loving father or mother. Indeed in Hebrews 12:6 we are told that "whom the Lord loveth He chasteneth", and that chastening is a sign of relationship. So the loving, caring parent will chasten the child. No delight will be taken in this act, and it must be carried out in a restrained and calm way. Whatever form it takes, the child must be made aware of the cause and why the correction is necessary.

The responsibility to honour parents

"Honour thy father and thy mother: that thy days may be long upon the land which the Lord thy God giveth thee" (Exod 20:12).

It is possible for children to obey parents, but not to honour them. They may carry out their wishes, but show by their attitude that they have no respect for their mother or father. Increasingly nowadays this is to be seen even in young children, and that is why we do not leave this subject until we deal with the teenage years.

It is equally important, however, that parents live in a way which earns the honour and respect of their children. Children are closer to parents than anyone else. They see at close range how the home is ordered, and they listen intently to all the conversations which take place, understanding more than most parents realise. In the home there are no outside on-lookers, and children are quick to pick up inconsistencies in their parents' actions, for example the excuse

Children are quick to pick up inconsistencies

that a mother cannot attend the prayer meeting because she is 'not too well' and then proceed to carry out tasks which require greater effort than going to pray with the Christians; the excuse that a father is too busy with work when the child knows that this only seems to be true of evenings when there are prayer or Bible teaching meetings to attend. Live before your children in such a way that inconsistencies are not glaringly obvious, and thus cause a lack of respect as the children grow and begin to understand what they see around them.

One of the clear commands of the Lord

The wise child will, however, always treat its parents with respect, no matter what kind of parents they have been. This is one of the clear commands of the Lord and is unconditional. Children are not told to honour their parents because they are worthy of honour. They are instructed to do this because the Lord would have it so.

A promise is attached to this commandment. In the case of the Israelites it was long life in the land of Canaan, and thus full enjoyment of all the good things provided by the Lord for them. This verse is quoted in Ephesians 6:3 where it obviously does no not refer to Canaan. For the Christian the promise is of a quality of life given as recompense for treating parents with honour.

A final word

Many parents feel that the responsibility of bringing up children is a task for which they are ill prepared. No amount of reading or education in the theory of parenthood can equip a mother and father for the realities of the situation. To look at a new born baby and realise that you have been charged with a responsibility which will be yours for years ahead, if the Lord will, is a daunting prospect.

And yet when it comes to the day to day issues, a mother knows instinctively how to protect and preserve her children. Similarly a father feels that he knows what is right and wrong for his child.

This must not, however, blind us to the fact that we must turn to the Scriptures to learn what the Lord would have us do. Solomon looked back to his early days and remembered a father who taught him: "Let thine heart retain my words: keep my commandments, and live" (Prov 4:4). Here is good advice for any parent. No matter how young a child may be, always seek to live before it in a manner which you would like your child to remember. Even in the home there is a sense in which parents are always on display. They are always being watched and their words are remembered.

Live in a manner which you would like your child to remember

It would be so sad if a child's early recollections were of anger and disputes, of parents whose spiritual life was obviously a sham, a front behind which there was no substance. Far better when the word of parents can be remembered as good advice for life in today's society and for living as a Christian in this godless age.

In that way we will have found the answer to the question with which we commenced this booklet: "How shall we order the child?" The answer of the angel to Manoah was that the word of God should be obeyed. For us the answer to the question remains the same. Put Scripture into practice and this can only be for the good of the home, for the good of the parents, and for the good of the child.

the john ritchie

family series

ISBN No. 0 946351 67 8

Typeset & Print: John Ritchie Ltd., 40 Beansburn, Kilmarnock, KA3 1RH

www.johnritchie.co.uk email: sales@johnritchie.co.uk

Illustrations: J. Glen